Being Adopted

Stephanie Herbert

Child Welfare League of America
Washington, DC

Child Welfare League of America, Inc.
440 First Street, NW, Suite 310, Washington, DC 20001-2085

CURRENT PRINTING (last digit)
10 9 8 7 6 5 4 3 2 1
Printed in the United States of America

ISBN # 0–87868–478–6

To my adoptive family,
with love.

When I was in
my mother's stomach
I must have felt lonely.

When I was born
my mother probably said
I was cute.

❧

But I didn't come out of the hospital with my mother. She said it would be okay if someone adopted me.

First my adoptive parents had to sign some papers.

Then they could adopt me and take me to their home.

It didn't feel too good to be away from my birth mother. I cried a lot because I missed her.

Now I'm seven years old. Sometimes I think about what my mother looks like and where she lives. I wonder if I have any brothers or sisters.

I live in a nice home now. My adoptive Mom and Dad love me. They give me new clothes to wear and healthy food to eat. We go to church together on Sundays.

When I'm older I hope I will see my birth mother. My adoptive parents said that would be nice.

I love my adopted mother and father and I am thankful for their love.